LIVE FROM
THE TIKI LOUNGE

LIVE FROM
THE TIKI LOUNGE

ANGELA WILLIAMS

MAYAPPLE PRESS 2008

Published by   MAYAPPLE PRESS
              408 N. Lincoln St.
              Bay City, MI 48708
              www.mayapplepress.com

ISBN 978-0932412-706

ACKNOWLEDGMENTS

I'd like to thank those who helped make this book possible.
I have great respect and gratitude for Judith Kerman and Amee Schmidt of
Mayapple Press, both keen guides on this book's journey.

My thanks to the editors of the journals and publications in which these
poems first appeared, sometimes in slightly different forms: Hale-Bopp, *Mississippi Review*; On the Corner of Vine & Locust, *GSU Review*; Field's Edge,
Emily Dickinson Prize Anthology; Plums, *Sky Magazine*; What was Mine,
Writer's Voice; You and the Ides of March, At the Edge of the Platte, Rough-
Legged Hawk, and Notes on the History of Prostitution, *Dunes Review*;
Maples on Fire, and At the Edge of the Platte appeared in the *Glen Arbor
Sun*. Almost Savages, is forthcoming in MOCAD's *Detroit: Stories*.

My sincere appreciation goes out to the supportive membership of Michigan Writers, Inc. with special thanks to Anne-Marie Oomen for her encouragement and brightness of spirit. I have unbounded gratitude for Mike
Callaghan.

Cover designed by Judith Kerman. Book designed and typset by Amee
Schmidt with titles in Lithos Pro and text in Maiandra GD.

CONTENTS

FIELD'S EDGE, MID-SEPTEMBER

The wind is not yet brutal as I dream.
Tonight I could be anyone's Venus,
framed by blood red sumac
and field corn waiting for
its shocks to be made fodder.
These breasts, hips, and ripe thoughts
could melt the coronas
around the moon itself.

I want time to let me be
the figurehead on a Viking ship,
an albatross to no one,
a Titian nude painted
on a bomber as a '40s pin-up girl
looking over my shoulder
as the currents lift and
there's no going back.

The point of no return is
a fresh tattoo on my heart,
a moon-dog before the killing frost.
I woke to the pale moon's hollow
departure to make a covenant
with morning doves because
faith comes more easily
to birds who plan to leave in autumn.

These next days will be
for stacking wood, piling deadfall.
Each slab is the wing of a grackle,
pairs of goldfinches,
plum flesh of a scarlet tanager,
the nape of a ring-necked pheasant.
We will hear their songs as their
flags unfold in each night's fire.

"If you fall from a great height into a vat of vegetable soup, you'll get a carrot in your ear. But you'll get much more than that."
—The Old Farmer's Almanac, *September 2006*

IN ANTICIPATION OF A FALSE HARVEST MOON

Jupiter is at its greatest height
and I want you.
As it lowers to its perigee
the Milky Way will split
in half, nearly clean-lined.
Its cut will be as quick as

the breath before a first kiss.
Two nights from now you'll
be driving home. I know
you'll see the moon
rising only to the horizon
and you'll marvel at its bounty.

But I'll know it's not yet time for the
killing frost, not time for empty trees.

YOU AND THE IDES OF MARCH:
A LOVE POEM TO WINTER

The morning I decided to leave
the sky was in between
Wedgewood and Wyeth.

All the trees were
pretending to be birches.

I ran through your dreams
in black and white,
an Ansel Adams print.

My lungs burst.
I grabbed saplings for balance.
It was a dry snow.

The woods grew thicker,
darker, as if morning was

never again to wake us.
I could hear no birds, nothing but the
pounding of what once was my heart.

THE LATER BIRD

You already have
your passport.
What you'll need
to leave safely,
cautiously, might
surprise you.

Take only a sliver
of the afternoon
sun on your cheek
leaning over me or
against me. I'll need
the rest of the light

to get through winter
after you've gone.

CAST-OFFS

We're a month beyond the first killing
frost and I need crows
to pick up debris falling

from the pewter sky like so many
steel shavings, carrion
as careless souvenirs

years and miles away
as if it hadn't mattered.
Perhaps it didn't really.

I tied a brocaded ribbon to a violinist's
bow the night he asked me to
name his cats who are by now dead.

Twenty years later I'm left with a
lover on safari with his wife.
And I can't breathe without him.

TO PERSEPHONE AS A MAN IN THE 21ST CENTURY

I prefer waltzes in the morning.
Strauss at seven, or so.
I wear a bell-shaped gown,
glide across a gleaming floor in your arms.
It can never be, but I feel your hand at my waist

remembering you once led me
away from myself so completely
our skin disappeared.

Before you return home
you'll choose a bauble at some
bazaar, hide it in your pocket
for your hand to graze its slightness.
I'll feel the rush up my spine as you take flight.

CHECKED BAGGAGE

I know the contents of your exile valise
from the litany, *I packed my*
grandmother's suitcase and in it I put...
I knew you'd pack holy water,
its level still full after I washed my mother's feet
the day she turned septic, the day I burned
sandalwood incense I bought
at the corner store when I went
for coffee and a paper,
the reassurance of knowing I'm still here.

Don't forget the menu from dinner
prepared by a murderer my sister dated:
an English roast thickly marinated
with fresh garlic, cumin,
balsamic vinegar, and cracked
black pepper seared, served rare
with morels flash sautéed with linguine
and crisp green beans. The posture of lunacy
was absent from my kitchen
the week before I saw him on the news.
He'd killed his stepfather over a jar of pickles.

I'll slip in the wingspan of a crow
and Lake Michigan high stepping through
a storm, preferably in spring.
You might place the light of a disappearing
sun in November carefully under the
promises I've never made to you.
I'll roll up the dreams of sisters next to the
guilt bought as a souvenir of their loathing
and the lessons I didn't know I was learning
when I witnessed their failures, their pains.

HALE-BOPP 3/26/97

(for my mother on her birthday)

You'd seen the comet in the east
in the morning
before the sun had finally risen, unknowingly.
Night viewing was too late.
You were tired.
It was unsafe, too cold,
not your idea of a good time.
It was easier to watch it on the news.
So I waited like I had for so many years
until you'd gone to bed to slip out of the house.

I waded into the silence of your open yard
to lay on my back, the house quieter than the black sky
and April approaching through the pines.
I lay on the snow imagining what it is to die,
not of the cold itself, but after;
the stainless steel drawer in the morgue,
a chilled sheet unwelcome in winter.
I lit a cigarette and watched its breath
close around my own,
drew ribbons of smoke into my chest,
and let them go as
Rubenesque ghosts waltzing after cordials.

Each glint that moved became someone
else's eyes asking to be remembered;
pinholes shuttering our own
version of eclipse. I am dismayed
about the naming of stars.
You can do it for under a hundred dollars
with a form from the *Farmers' Almanac*
and love doesn't stick around
long enough to learn the miracle of clichés.
Star-crossed, indeed.

We are the simple crap-shoot chances
taken by everyone who passed before us:
running late and taking the second boat,
a locked door, the sun forcing us out
into its warmth, a bullet through the
Sacred Heart of Jesus carried in a shirt pocket,
a tap on the shoulder requesting a dance.

LETTING IN MY MOTHER

I sat with her at lunch.
We talked.
I asked the right questions.
She said she didn't love my father
until after I was born.
She weighed 106 soaking wet,
still had her figure at age 43.
What is love?

She wouldn't tell me.
Have to figure it out by accident.
Hold the ball until you can't stand it any more.
Take a bus and say no thank you, anyway.
Buy a cowboy hat and dream.
Or visit a pawn shop somewhere in Oklahoma
for wedding bands and talk about Elvis.
And let it make sense to you.
Let it make sense to you.
And she told me she still thought
about could-have-beens: that man
in the photo she carried in the back
of her wallet until she gave it to me
a day before her coma, four
days before she died. *No one
else will understand this part of me.*

He glowed when he walked
into Uncle Pete's house on Oliver Street.
She was in love but moved away for summer.
He showed up on an Indian motorcycle
at the corner by Beulah Drug
the night of my parents' first date.
She told him to leave—
something about propriety.
He got a room at the Crystal Hotel.
Aunt Gladys gave him maids' rates.
In the morning
my mother went to his room

but he was gone.
She lay on the bed trying to smell him
for more than two hours.

Uncle Pete died in 1969.
I remember.
I tried to blow the candles out
at the funeral in the church.
Perhaps it was a party for a child.
The sight of that man made my mother
run out of the room.
She said she couldn't breathe,
didn't want a businessman to know
she'd settled for a dumb farmer.
My father wasn't stupid.
He must have known she was ashamed.
He made the man laugh and
they talked about the war.

I wore a blue dress and pounded on the door.
She stayed in the bathroom where
there was a scale that told her
fortune for a quarter.

MAPLES ON FIRE

I could give you faith by painting what's outside my window.
But I won't. I gave it up at seventeen.
A portrait of the Virgin Mary was left unfinished.
Her cheeks were too red. They were flashes of leaves
on a dark wet road waiting to be crushed,
their spine, then veins, then all.

I caught a glimpse of a child's face among the scattered
confetti, hot and cold from playing too hard in the damp
air. I could hear a throaty cough, some peels of laughter,
feel the sodden insisted-upon gloves caked with mud.

I wanted to surround the Madonna with the light that cuts
through stands of trees from clouds as a warning,
a sign of divinity from roadside bracken.
When my sister was small she said,
*That kind of sunlight means that someone is
being taken away from us, that beauty is owned by gravity.*

PLUMS

Peasant fruit faces
out when the
woodcock's breast
is peeled.

No pulp surrounds
its heart. Hollow
bones hold fourth
position in flight.

The space between
shot and echo
measures how
fine a touch can be.

Before blood and
sweetness come
before juice has
time to run down

fingers, its red edge
reminds the sun on
the neck of a boy; it is
time for his first kiss.

PLUTO RECLASSIFIED

It all comes down to
the wonder of what
more can be
snatched away from us.

My very educated mother
just served us nothing...
No more pickles or pork-chops
or pudding. Not even plums.

It's now just the last stop
on the Copernican A-train,
before the vacancy sign
at our universe's edge.

There's no time to
give her your number.
No chance to utter
an eloquent goodbye.

The next time you
see her she'll be
appearing live from
the Tiki Lounge in

some beach town,
translating drink orders
for the summer
Mexican boys who work

the tarps in the
orchards. She'll have
a coconut bra
thematically stowed

in her jacket pocket to
give to the barmaid if the
ceiling is high enough for
dancing on the bar.

NIGHT OF THE TERRAPINS

I don't own the memory of the
box full of eggs from
the Betsie River bed my sisters
placed on the clothes dryer
for heat. I remembered instead
the box with edges peeled
then slid up on the black tarpaper
roof of our half-finished house,
sun urging them into the world,
a hundred faint scratches
as they hatched then clamored
to the edges. My sisters
caught them before they
reached the eaves and took
them back to the river after dinner.

Today two trucks were on the shoulder
of M-22. Men circled then speared
a three-foot snapper's skull. The beheading
of an American civilian at the hands of
Iraquis repeated on the news this morning.

I can't shake their posture,
owned by my mother the day I spoke
my first word: *why.*
A June school program for
my brother. She was rushing.
I was in the middle of her
bed as she readied. A fitted gingham
shirtdress, heels damn near stilettos.
At the bottom of East Hill our
'63 Valiant wagon shook when
she braked to avoid a snapper.
She got out, took a shovel from
the back, pounded in its head,
and scooped it into the car.
I couldn't stop watching it die.

A World without Venus

I will not accept assignment into the collective Eve,
become part of the mounded cross-hatched hay stacks
in the foreground of a more important sky.

I will dig deep enough to find the one-tusked sweetness
of a sandalwood elephant who stayed in my pocket
until that August afternoon when the field caught fire,
falling into the thigh brushing grass as I ran.
It was all turned over in years we could not lie fallow.

We became golden sod, whorled rolls cut up and out,
Picasso's breasts depicted in a gruesome dialect
because this is what we've come to.

Reverence

Saturday morning
seated beside a prayer rug
sun from an Eastern window
found thirty two Cerulean

blue eyes tying woven edges
of odd October heat
to tails of ponies born
just for princes to ride.

FATHER DREAM

Last night the bodies
were stacked
outside my barn
next to the fallow
garden. This time
they were Picasso's
cold blues and yellows
and I heard their skin
drying in the dark.

In the field behind the
rabbits' shed a stake
held a man with hollows
for eyes, pleading.
No sound came.
I turned away.
My limbs fell from
my body to the frozen
ground. I could do nothing.

I have to give up looking
for you, making myself
believe I see you. When
I catch a fragment of
your shadow out of the
corner of my eye I want
to be brave, to call
your name in a clear voice,
to ask you to wait.

In Lieu of the Eucharist in Appalachia

The maples have all
been milked. The last
ice has wedged
into the horse-toothed
bark of pines.

I am so
hollowed by the
sweetness
of May's underbelly.
If I could choose

the time to die it
would be now as the
lace of birches brushes
the sky and no god
would be the wiser.

I don't know
who will find me
first. I'd prefer you
because you'd go so far
as to lay bread on the shell

of my body as sin eaters*
do, and you'd take your
time on the solid crust,
leaving a wake of sharp crumbs
broken over my stilled chest.

---

*   *Sin-eating entailed the literal acceptance of another's sins through the taking of food offered in the presence of that person's corpse. It was practiced throughout Europe in the Middle Ages. The earliest sin-eaters were the old or the poor of the village held in contempt by their neighbors. They were called when one of the God-fearing breathed his last and faced Eternal Judgment. Since the Church frequently punished those who displeased it through excommunication, there were many who died without benefit of Last Rites or there were no priests available. The outcasts were offered a coin and food, often just a piece of salted bread, placed on the chest of the deceased; in return, they accepted the sins committed by that person into their own souls.*

MAYDAY EVE:
INSOMNIA AND FLOWERS

It's four a.m. The lilacs hedging
this house suffocate the thin spring air.

I pace the hall like the senile,
my grandmother twenty years dead
among them. I can smell the women
at the home, in stiff cotton
housecoats who've splashed on old
cologne, daubed the napes of their
necks, the fine folds of oniony skin
on their wrists, behind their knees.
I can't recall their names or faces.

Maybe I never knew them, never knew her.
I want the moon to be full now, this instant.

I could trace the raised velvet
wall-paper perfectly, if asked.
Each stem, curl, and petal remains
in the memory of my fingers.
A grave leafless wind sheds frail
light and charges lilies for my guilt.
In June they will ripen and hover over
the pond like small bright fruit
Ophelia could have eaten.

If the sky was clear I would settle for
the brittle illumination of stars.

FRANKIE WOULD'VE FLOWN ME

Oh who are we
years past the real Vegas?

Tonight a perfect moon
hangs bemused
at top dead center
in the eastern
Caesar's Palace
blue at twilight sky.

I have been that moon
on days I forgot,
dismissing its light.
Those days that build a life,
lead us in the direction pathing
and drawing us nearer the most

definite "x" marking the spot from
which we chose to stray.

Going Gently

Tonight was the first clean-lined sunset of May. A hundred
miles up the coast you're committing the points of light
to memory to paint when your flowers are buried in snow.

I counted eighteen sunspots before the sun flattened
into the water, collapsed into a silent paper squash.
I listened for that final groan, some sigh of music.

If I leave here early enough, on the way home past you
at dawn I'll have strip motels lit in the same pink neon.
The air will be cold and wet enough for me to know what loam is.

As the breath escaped I knew the practices and theories
of devotion now elude me, perhaps have always eluded me.

En Route

The damp and the dark excuse me.
As I walk through the pines we planted
I long for days stooped over furrows
dust covered and breathing heat.
We would pray for this
rain then, as we placed
each tap root facing true north
to sleep in the earth as we did in our beds
aligned under the stars we would not name.

If I could be Kokoschka's *Bride of the Wind*
the seasons might never matter;
only the swirling lapis of the sky
and my embrace as a haven for your fears.
I wouldn't let you go. And my heart
wouldn't shatter into sharp shards of
cobalt as if someone put a stone
through Chagall's windows.
Doves and floating lovers smashed into razors.

Tonight there is no time or desire
to discern the sting of sharp rain
as a wind-driven baptism.
I cross ridge to rut daring to keep
a fraction of you, of what had become
part of me, most of me. When I get to
the edge I'll stop to listen for your breath.
But there is nothing the wind
and the rain won't eventually take from us.

ONE SHADE OF INDIGO

Your eyes do not belong to you.
You borrowed them from the sky
or found them on the street
one rainy afternoon, rescued them
just as a battered taxi rounded the corner
heading your way. You scooped them up
and tucked them tenderly into your
breast pocket before they realized their danger.

Those aren't your eyes because they hold
truths told by oceans you've never seen.
You took them in lieu of my heart.
You never called again. I didn't expect it.
I hung a saint around my neck
instead of hoping for your answer.

Your eyes belong to someone who knew
the depth of blue lines on water and
whistled the mating calls of bright birds.
He left them on the beach with his shoes.
It was sunset and the streaks across the
lake and dune grass were all he wanted
to remember. You picked them up
the next morning beach-combing for coins.

When you find something that isn't lost
it becomes part of you and you become
one *milagro* exchanged for another's wishes.

I'm the Girl in the Window

You say rain
came so hard
it stung your
cheek. You held

my gaze but
walked on.
You stopped
at the corner

before you crossed
the street,
turned back.
When you arrived

at the café
I was gone.
So you returned
to the corner.

Where you'd stood
a blue
coupe had
crashed right into

the wrought-iron
streetlamp. You
say you
couldn't forget me

because I saved
your life and
I didn't
even know it.

PERMIT ME TO TEND THIS SPOT

It takes the right light to see what
has been forgotten; the glint of a
flag holder from a war so long ago
there can't possibly be any survivors.

Some prefer to be forgotten.
Not here, not on this hill
with the view of the valley
and further. Lake Michigan
when the leaves are down
before it snows.

This place meant hope for legacy;
for someone who'd come
to trim the forsythia and
place a smooth stone by your name.
There's no one left who knew you,
which dreams you realized,
what broke your heart,
the color of your favorite sky.

I chose my barrenness.
My best hope: someone will do
me the same favor. Someone who
will not know me by the tattoo
of an angel posed as Andromeda
on my left shoulder, or by my voice

calling from the porch, or because
I can't keep out of the rain. I fear
this won't be possible. I will be abandoned
beneath the chill of winter. *Look for me.*

ROUGH-LEGGED HAWK

It wasn't until I knew what he was;
when I named him, he left.
I've been by each day since
but his post at the field's edge
remains empty. My sentry
has left for the Arctic, finally.

And I think it's his fault that my
dreams have been of the Holocaust,
harvested tomatoes overflowing in
bushel baskets and wooden lugs
(a perfect one perched on a dry stem),
and the essence of my life on fire.

All I can do is search for the leashes
and collars for the dogs because if
they flee unreined they'll never return.

04-11-05
On the 60th anniversary of Buchenwald concentration
camp's liberation

On the Corner of Vine & Locust

It wasn't just a shop kept by a pale
red-haired woman so fair you'd
swear you'd seen her face in the moon.

It was rumored the five pearl buttoned
             full-trained, whiter than a sail
in the memory of a July lake, clearly
             Victorian wedding gowns
marked *sold*   hung in ascension
    flat on the back   wall of the back room
             beyond a small oak bridge
        over a goldfish pond bordered
by full-bosomed skirted 1920's
        swimwear in faded red and inky navy
all belonged to her but had never been worn.

She tried to sell me strands of beads
left over from Mardi Gras in New Orleans.
She said they'd hung at the neck
        of a king she danced with until she forgot
        she once had feet.
But I only had enough for wool gloves.
She quietly asked if I'd seen
her cat outside before I entered.
        No, I lied
 and spent it all on baubles;
 the brightness of imaginary romance
        as penance for what I couldn't tell her
and had to walk past again when I left.

It lay there, March rain soaking in
as if it was just a clump of muddied snow
at street's edge; a half-brown half-white shard
             kicked off a car's wheel well.
Something that didn't mean a damn thing.
Certainly nothing to be remembered
except that it was hers, the crushed

figure at the curb, its mouth still
            agape and fangs poised for its
tenth life biting air like the
wrinkled hide of a pomegranate.

I see it when I close my eyes,
when I dig my nails
            deeper than I should
but not as deep as I can
            into the palm of my hand scraping
      temporary extensions
into what began as uncertain deadlines at best.

Step Four:
Taking a Moral Inventory

I chew juniper berries, roll their barky sheaths
to the cleft of my palette. The pine dives

with a breath to a forgotten black hole
that came before gin and waking.

Even strangers in the street know the only thing left
after smashing the glass into the fire is the stem.

I can't even hope for original bitterness.
I read van Gogh had a fetish for cypress trees.

He hunched behind them out of the yellow
Arles afternoons, waited for their branches
to whisper, rubbed against them, and wept.

ALMOST SAVAGES

The only blue I've seen for weeks is this body,
the color of my winter sky in plumage, a jay

fresh-killed for my assumption of doubt
for spring's awakening. And it will be

months until there is haven again for any of us.
Months until warmth is pliant in lake beds when

small fish will scatter away from my steps.
How many moonfish would the river hold

if you squeezed the banks together for an instant?
Each April I think of my father's smelt runs, the inky

rimed artesian creek lined shoulder to shoulder three
men deep pressing in with nets and lanterns. Kerosene

hung in the piercing air. The rush of silver thicker than
a slot machine's payment. He'd bring his pails into

the kitchen before sunrise, line the table with yesterday's
paper, hand us each a shining knife, and pour the smelt

into a pile, some still alive, their flat eyes breathing.
It is not a field of poppies, this death. Nor is it the

shadow of a black willow, its head downcast unless
the wind builds coming in from the big lake. Steeling

from bleakness takes as much as hurtling upstream.
These willow leaves now, damp as nervous fingers

splayed across the fractured sidewalk are the jay's
feathers scattered from the cats' elation. The headless

corpse, wanton by the cellar door, their usual modus operandi.
First blood at the throat, then sliced clean up the belly.

31

The Emptiest Lines

I've become bare
November fields
cleared of
everything sweet or
dear or soft of
summer.

Even October's
cotton milkweed
flags have
disappeared.
Probably gone south
with fickle and greedy birds;

fleeing tenants who've
taken the last light-bulb.

OBBLIGATO

North, not yet to Sleeping Bear
past half-shorn cornfields
cow barns begin to clot
against November's slate blue sky.

In this bitter cold it's as
if I never dreamed
Jesus riding in my
truck one day in summer.

It was raining. Jesus, there beside
me in the cab and we headed south.
I pulled over to check the trailer behind us.
My father was in it with hay, and drinking
whiskey from a jug, singing
"You are my sunshine..."
Sun washed everything: the road dirt smell
of my hands, the liquor, the hay, my bones.
Jesus told me to get in.
He asked if everything was all right.
I told him I didn't want what was given to me.

In the seam of the sky each day
as the sun opens on a certain rise
lined by poplars, I am reminded
of each love gone wrong or just gone.

IN HOPPER'S "CHOP SUEY"

We're the couple in the darkened corner.
You've just finished your soup.

I've just told you of my penchant for the
"I'm a Little Teapot" song as a child.
You decide to order a sake.

You smile, then tell me you still
want to live in a tree-house.

The afternoon hangs on a high clothesline;
flapping yellowed honest muslin. I tell you
I haven't slept. I stayed up to write thick

lines on the beauty of negative space and how
I lost something once. You've nothing left to say.

EXPLODING VEGAS

(for Big Joe)

If you were Elvis
you would, perhaps,
pilot an ice cutter
or be known
as a regular
at the Landmark
sitting at a
corner nickel
slot, awaiting

the rare glimpse
of Howard Hughes
whose scepter
has since given
way, imploded
for the sole
purpose of
becoming a
parking lot.

I'd want to
serve you
god-awful
Jim Beam,
I think, because
it's what
you'd order.

And if the lights
flashed and the
bells rang
I'd want to be
there with you.
Winters are long enough
and cold enough, my love.

05-05-05 Upon watching the National Geographic channel's
special on implosions of classic Vegas hotels.   35

EARLY SATURDAY

When I saw Georgia O'Keefe's
"Purple Hills near Abiquiu"
I saw you sleeping.
The ridges were
your thighs
drawn up,
a soft haunch
draped with dusty linen
in the morning light.
The folds held sinew
wrapping your ribs, hips and knees.
Out of view
was your bared
foot trying to find
its way back
under the sheet or
a way to
completely disrobe you.

NOTES ON THE HISTORY OF PROSTITUTION ON THE 500TH BIRTHDAY OF MICHELANGELO'S *DAVID*

(for a stonecutter who should have lived in ancient Greece)

If the soles of my shoes
wrote "follow me"
in the dust of the
streets or up and over
a ravine to privacy
and all we would hear
is the break of each
wave in entire unison
to each our own
heart's beat, would you?

And if you finally chose
to carve into stone,
would you be readied
for the form borne
with each tup of
kevel in to chisel's end,
becoming each
breath taken, each
drop from your brow
hours in to the edge of
the night you own,
when alone with stars
as guests at your window?

It would be solstice.
I would sit for you
on the right as
Magdalene. I would
be your holy grail.
It would suit your
ideal, then eternity's
ideal. It would not be
my feet walking away
by their own choosing.

At the Edge of the Platte

Two fishermen blind passed
two coho in the shallows.

A beech leaf crisped its edges
enough to become a canoe,
earnest and giddy on its way.

I wanted to be in its stern,
your rumpled head spotted
by sun flecking through the
redding maples, resting in my lap.

WHAT WAS MINE

(on the way to a father's funeral in March)

I don't know how many bodies there were
along the road heading south.
They were deer carcasses; picked-clean hides
dry as the remains of winter wheat.
Their blood seeped into the soil
turning it black as moonless nights.
Nothing was left for the crows to steal.

Crossing the Looking Glass River
I thought of bayous and how many Mardi Gras
I've never known. I'd so much rather dance
naked, drunk, and draped in beads than be reminded
I can't say anything new about fear or water or love
other than they can hold the darkness like the edge
of a hood and mere possibilities keep me breathless.

If I look closely and quickly enough as I travel
I see the eyes of anyone who's ever mattered
in between the trees, hear their voices under the call
of birds coming home from far away.
Somehow the sense birds make of things
tells secrets that never were;
the outstretched wings of mating cranes,
the screams of hawks and owls before daybreak,
a murmuration of starlings against a morning sky.

With each passing mile I want to close my eyes,
stay anchored, pretend it never happened,
that this trek, this journey is not real. I remember standing
bare in an art class except for a long strand of pearls.
There were no windows and I kept thinking to myself,
I will never get cold, I must never get cold.

About the Author

Angela Knauer Williams grew up in northern Michigan and lives there now with her family where the trains used to run at night through the valley. She studied creative writing and theatre at Western Michigan University, and now works in the cherry industry in Leelanau County. She's prone to bringing home feral kittens that are incapable of developing social skills and only ordering vanilla ice cream at Dairy King.

Her first book *With a Cherry on Top*, published by Mayapple Press in 2006, featured poems, stories, recipes and essays about Michigan cherries from various regional writers.

OTHER RECENT TITLES FROM MAYAPPLE PRESS:

Claire Keyes, *The Question of Rapture*, 2008
        Paper, 72 pp, $14.95 plus s&h
        ISBN 978-0932412-690
Judith Kerman and Amee Schmidt, eds., *Greenhouse: The First 5 Years of the Rustbelt Roethke Writers' Workshop*, 2008
        Paper, 78 pp, $14.95 plus s&h
        ISBN 978-0932412-683
Cati Porter, *Seven Floors Up*, 2008
        Paper, 66 pp, $14.95 plus s&h
        ISBN 978-0932412-676
Rabbi Manes Kogan, *Fables from the Jewish Tradition*, 2008
        Paper, 104 pp, $19.95 plus s&h
        ISBN 978-0932412-669
Joy Gaines-Friedler, *Like Vapor*, 2008
        Paper, 64 pp, $14.95 plus s&h
        ISBN 978-0932412-652
Jane Piirto, *Saunas*, 2008
        Paper, 100 pp, $15.95 plus s&h
        ISBN 978-0932412-645
Joel Thomas Katz, *Away*, 2008
        Paper, 42 pp, $12.95 plus s&h
        ISBN 978-0932412-638
Tenea D. Johnson, *Starting Friction*, 2008
        Paper, 38 pp, $12.95 plus s&h
        ISBN 978-0932412-621
Brian Aldiss, *The Prehistory of Mind*, 2008
        Paper, 76 pp, $14.95 plus s&h
        ISBN 978-0932412-614
Andy Christ, *Philip and the Poet*, 2008
        Paper, 26 pp, $12.95 plus s&h
        ISBN 978-0932412-607
Jayne Pupek, *Forms of Intercession*, 2008
        Paper, 102 pp, $15.95 plus s&h
        ISBN 978-0932412-591
Elizabeth Kerlikowske, *Dominant Hand*, 2008
        Paper, 64 pp, $14.95 plus s&h
        ISBN 978-0932412-584

For a complete catalog of Mayapple Press publications, please visit our website at *www.mayapplepress.com*. Books can be ordered direct from our website with secure on-line payment using PayPal, or by mail (check or money order). Or order through your local bookseller.